— PEOPLE TO KNOW —

ANN RICHARDS

Politician, Feminist, Survivor

Dorothy Schainman Siegel

ENSLOW PUBLISHERS, INC.

44 Fadem Road	P.O. Box 38
Box 699	Aldershot
Springfield, N.J. 07081	Hants GU12 6BP
U.S.A.	U.K.

Library of Congress Cataloging-in-Publication Data

Siegel, Dorothy Schainman.
    Ann Richards : politician, feminist, survivor / Dorothy Schainman Siegel.
        p. cm. — (People to know)
    Includes bibliographical references (p.) and index.
    Summary: Covers the public and private life of the second female
governor of Texas, from her childhood in the small town of Lakeview
through her one term in the state's highest office.
    ISBN 0-89490-497-3
        1. Richards, Ann, 1933– — Juvenile literature. 2. Governors—Texas—
Biography—Juvenile literature. [1. Richards, Ann, 1933– . 2. Governors.
3. Women— Biography.] I. Title. II. Series.
F391.4.R53S59 1996
976.4'063'092—dc20
    [B]   95-25542
                                                                            CIP
                                                                             AC
    Printed in the United States of America

10 9 8 7 6 5 4 3 2 1

Illustration Credits: Compliments of Governor's Office Archives, Austin,
Texas, p. 4; Ann Richards' Personal Collection, pp. 12, 31; Photo by Ruth
Welbes, p. 21; Prints & Photographs Collection, The Center for American
History, The University of Texas at Austin, p. 35; Photo by Susan Gaetz,
pp. 42, 64, 69, 73, 82, 85, 93, 96, 98; The Dallas Morning News/Judy
Walgren, p. 77.

Cover Illustration: Compliments of Governor's Office Archives, Austin,
Texas

Contents

Ann Richards

Introduction

Atlanta, Georgia, was the site of the Democratic National Convention during the summer of 1988. Everywhere, television screens showed the great auditorium of the Omni Hotel as a mass of color. Posters, banners, flags, ribbons, every style of hat—flashy or plain—met viewers' eyes. They saw excited delegates throwing fistfuls of confetti in the air. Naturally, the colors of choice were red, white, and blue.

Silver and gold sparkles twinkled under the lights while flags and banners were raised up and down on poles, or waved wildly before the cameras.

The delegates were in a festive mood. They shouted campaign slogans and sang pop, rock, and folk songs at the top of their lungs, pausing to cheer for each speaker.

When a voice boomed out of the public address system with a new announcement, people calmed down a bit. They had been eagerly waiting for the next speech. As the handsome, silver-haired speaker stepped up to the microphone, a hush came over the expectant audience as they waited for her to begin. This speaker was Ann Richards.

Ann had become a nationally-known political figure in 1984 when she had eloquently seconded the nomination of Walter F. Mondale for president of the United States.

After his stunning loss, Ann was appointed to the steering committee of the Democratic party's policy committee. Her considerable energy and intelligence were so impressive that party leaders chose her to deliver the 1988 keynote address.

On that day, Ann was so nervous that she had to clutch her glass of water with both hands to keep from spilling it.[1] But she delivered a memorable speech in her distinctive Texan twang. It was characterized by her hallmark qualities of passion and emotion. As usual, she leavened the speech with her special brand of humor—occasionally impish, sometimes biting, even sardonic. She teased [then] Vice President George Bush for some of the blunders he had made in his speeches. "Poor George, he can't help it—he was born with a silver foot in his mouth!" Her audience loved it.[2]

Early in her speech, Ann turned to more serious, feminist matters. "Twelve years ago, Barbara Jordan, another Texas woman . . . made the keynote address to this convention," she reminded the Atlanta delegates, "and two women in 160 years is about par for the course.

"But if you will give us a chance, we can perform. After all, Ginger Rogers did everything Fred Astaire did. She just did it backwards and in high heels."[3,4]

The audience roared its approval as Ann brought down the house. Many applauded until their palms stung before starting a chorus of ear-splitting whistles.

Women delegates of all races and nationalities grinned happily as they danced in celebration and hugged one another.

It wasn't very different from the responses Ann had been getting throughout her brief political career. By 1988 Ann had held elective office only thirteen years. But they were important and eventful years.

"Deep in the Heart of Texas"

Ann Richards began life in Central Texas on September 1, 1933. Originally named Dorothy Ann, she was born in Lakeview, a small town outside of Waco. It was a crossroads with a misleading name. There was no lake to view![1] Ann started near the bottom of the pole in a place that wasn't even on the map. She couldn't have known that one day she would reach the top—in her own home state.

Ann was the only child of Iona and Cecil Willis, who came from tiny Texan towns called Bugtussle and Hogjaw.[2] She still calls them Daddy and Mama. Her father drove a delivery truck for a pharmaceutical firm; her mother worked in a dry-goods store.

After their marriage, the Willises bought a small, one-bedroom house on an acre of land in Lakeview. Ann was born at home in that bedroom. Cecil and Iona were hard-working people who carefully watched their spending. They either banked their money or used it only for necessities.

Ann believes her mother would have liked more children. But Ann was born during the Great Depression, and times were hard. Her father once earned only $100 a month. When things got really bad, he had to accept a cut to $88.50.[3]

Her parents sometimes struggled to make ends meet, yet they managed to pay for "necessities" such as Ann's piano and public speaking lessons. They may have felt they wouldn't have been able to provide these activities if they had additional children. Since Cecil and Iona always wanted to give Ann everything they never had, she remained an only child.

Their large garden was one sign of the Willises' thriftiness. That's where they grew everything for the family table. They also raised chickens, ducks, and an occasional hog.

In another sign of thrift, Ann's mother made nearly all her clothes. A skilled seamstress, she often used flour or feed sacks for fabric, as most Lakeview mothers did during those years. When Ann was in a school play, Iona Willis made her costumes.

At school, Ann was always the youngest in her class. She can't say why, it just worked out that way. In fact, there were rarely more than fifteen kids in any one grade.

(All twelve grades were in one building.) She doesn't remember anything special about those years, except that she always spoke out in class. She admits this probably drove everyone crazy![4]

If her early school days didn't leave much of an impression on Ann, it might have been because teachers didn't demand much of pupils. Perhaps they didn't make classes compelling enough; we'll never know. In any event, it was all right with Ann. She wasn't especially good or bad at her studies. This didn't bother her parents either. As far as they were concerned, scholarship wasn't the most important thing in life. What they really valued was personality. Ann certainly had that. She still does!

Ann loved performing. Her parents encouraged her, but they weren't the only ones. Many of their neighbors also enjoyed watching Ann perform. It was a lesson she learned early in life: "People liked you if you told stories, if you made them laugh."[5] She often adds that everyone liked listening to her father's stories. He was, and still is, a gifted storyteller.

Cecil was also Ann's number one fan. "She entered everything that ever happened around [Lakeview]. I don't care what it was," he remembers. "She liked plays, all that entertainment stuff. I'd tell her, you can do whatever you want [to] do, honey, just get up and go after it."[6] Ann did just that and ended up in most of her

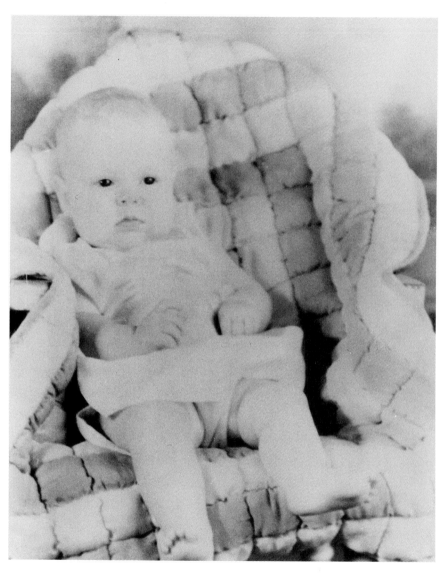

When Dorothy Ann Willis was born, her parents had no idea that their little baby would grow up to be governor of the state of Texas.

school's plays, usually in the lead because of the wonderful costumes her mother made for her.

There were other opportunities to perform at school. Along with several classmates, Ann took weekly public speaking lessons. They weren't very complicated; everyone memorized what Ann calls "little ditties" and poems. Later, they read these during a special program called a recital. She remembers cutting stories out of newspapers and magazines for her speeches. Ann did very well. Even as a "little bitty first grader," she learned to stand up and say her piece. It was a preview of the political performances that lay ahead.

At the same time that her folks tried to prepare Ann for a better future, they unconsciously set an example. Many years later she recalled the strong, unspoken message they gave her: The only thing of any real value in life is hard work. If she remembers anything about her childhood it is how hard her mother worked.[7]

When she was younger, Ann had her chores plus anything else her mother might ask her to do. It was how she was expected to learn to become responsible. For example, every week she cleaned an ivy plant that Iona had trained to cover a wall of the porch, polishing each dusty leaf with milk. Ann hated that chore and wondered who cared if the leaves stayed dusty. She certainly didn't![8] But she never rebelled, and the leaves generally gleamed after she finished that chore.

Ann usually played with friends after school, climbing trees or running barefoot on the dusty roads.

In fact, Ann went barefoot whenever possible. For one thing, it saved her school shoes. She knew that the more she wore them after school, the sooner they would wear out. Because Ann never walked when she could run, her father used to call her a perpetual motion machine.[9]

The neighborhood children often fought "chinaberry wars." Big chinaberry trees grew near Ann's house. In season they have lovely clusters of violet-colored, sweet-smelling blossoms. These flowers later turn into squishy yellow berries that kids would use as ammunition to hurl at each other.

After the *Wonder Woman* comics came out, Ann would pretend to be her favorite heroine when she climbed trees.

She also liked to shinny up to the garage roof with a rope she called her magic lariat. Holding onto it, she would jump off and land safely.

It was all part of a mind-set Ann got from her parents. As long as she believed she could do something, from jumping safely off the garage roof to winning a prize at a public speaking recital, there was a good chance that she would succeed at it. Iona added the proviso that whatever Ann did, she had to work at it and do the job right. That explains why her mother expected shiny, clean ivy leaves after Ann finished that particular chore. If any dust remained, Ann had to repeat her efforts until Iona was satisfied the ivy looked as nice as possible.

The same rule held for any other task. Iona's slogan could have been: "If it's worth doing, it's worth doing well." For instance, washing up after dinner meant that not one crumb could remain on a dish or in a skillet; otherwise, everything had to be thoroughly rewashed until it was sparkling clean. After her mother taught Ann to sew, the seams on a garment had to match perfectly. If not, she had to tear everything out and start all over again.

Ann learned these important lessons early on. Whatever she did had to be quality; otherwise, it wasn't worth doing. Still, Ann wouldn't want anyone feeling sorry for her. She wasn't a poor little girl who worked all the time. On the contrary, Ann says no one could have been as well loved as she had been by her parents. If anything, Cecil and Iona expected her to achieve. Trouble was, they couldn't put into words precisely what she should excel in. The older Willises weren't used to expressing themselves like that. So Ann never had a clue and had to pick up their hopes by osmosis.[10]

Along with instilling in Ann the belief that she could do whatever she set out to do, her father also encouraged her to question injustice, often setting an example for her. For instance, as a member of the Lakeview School Board, he helped to save the job of a teacher about to be dismissed because she was pregnant. Some board members felt she shouldn't continue teaching her fourth grade class once her condition became obvious.

This was too much for Cecil Willis. He stood up in exasperation and called the situation the most ridiculous thing he'd ever heard. The woman's husband was in the army, and she needed her salary to support herself. He convinced the board, and they voted to let her continue teaching for the rest of the school year.[11]

Ann often went fishing with her father, not just for fun but for food. They would go out late at night to set fishing lines between river banks. She helped place baited hooks along them hoping the bait would attract a big catfish. It was exciting and scary.

Sometimes, a full moon lit their way across the dark, quiet waters. Or they'd carry a lantern to inspect the lines, paddling their way through the darkness. With luck, there would be one or two meals on the hooks the next morning.

During those early years in Lakeview, Ann Willis Richards led a quiet, happy life. Then World War II began and her father was drafted into the United States Navy. The period that followed would have a memorable effect on Ann.

2

The World Opens Up

Ann remembers the evening before her father left for boot camp. She was nine years old and it was the first time she had ever seen him cry.

Ordinarily the Willises didn't hug and kiss a lot. But that evening Cecil hugged Ann hard and began to weep.

She didn't understand why he was going away. It certainly never occurred to her that she might never see her father again. So she hugged him back, and with her mother bravely waved him off the following day.

It wasn't long before they joined him in San Diego, California, where he was stationed. Before they left home, though, Iona went to a Waco business college where she learned to operate a mechanical calculator called a comptometer. The precursor of electronic calculators (computers), it could add, subtract, multiply, and divide. She could use this skill to support herself and Ann if Cecil's pay didn't cover their needs.

Ann remembers driving out West to be with him. Her mother killed and canned their chickens because she knew food would cost more in San Diego than it did in their little corner of Texas. They loaded the car with canned foods and their belongings, then strapped Iona's sewing machine in the trunk.

Life in San Diego differed a great deal from what Ann had known in the dusty backwoods of Lakeview, a *very* small town in comparison. Now, suddenly, the world began to open up.

First Ann and her mother had to find a place to stay. It wasn't easy. After all, there was a war on. Other people also needed housing, which was very scarce.

They first lived in a single room in the basement of a private home, where Cecil joined them on weekends. The room was so small that Ann slept on a cot and had to get up so that her father could get out the door when he returned to the naval base on Monday mornings.

After a while they found an apartment, renting for $30 a month. Ann still recalls how shocked her parents were by this amount of money.[1]

When Iona couldn't find work as a comptometer operator, she had Ann hand-letter a sign that read "Alterations and Dressmaking." After they placed it in front of their building, orders started coming in and Ann's mother began to take in sewing.

At the same time, Ann drank in the excitement of city life which was so different from what she had known back in Texas. For one thing, San Diego remains in her mind as the place where she ate her first doughnut. It was a whole new world.[2]

In San Diego, just going to the store for food was a new experience for Ann. Back in Texas, nearly everything they ate came from their garden, from fishing, and occasionally from hunting. (Her father taught Ann how to shoot and took her hunting when she was about nine.) Now if they wanted something for dinner, they would get the fixings from a grocery store.

After moving to San Diego, Ann's world broadened in other ways. Going to school was quite an eye-opener. In fact, that's where she learned how vast the world was. To get to Theodore Roosevelt Junior High, she had to take a bus and a trolley. There was no question of biking to school, it was all the way across town. First she walked about a block to the bus stop. After the bus dropped her off in the center of the city, she caught a streetcar to school.

It was an experience Ann never forgot, riding across a high trestle through Balboa Park and looking down on either side. She remembers the beautiful view, and thinking it was a forest. It was a long way from the dusty, flat country around Lakeview where Ann was born.

School was an equally memorable experience. Ann had never seen Spanish architecture before going west, and the school was built in that style. Made of light pastel stucco with a ceramic tile roof, it seemed like something out of the movies, also a far cry from Texas. So was the student body. Ann couldn't recall having seen so many different kinds of faces: African-American, Hispanic, Greek, Italian. No wonder Ann said later that going to school in Califoria in the early 1940s was like going to another country.

Although they were different colors and came from different backgrounds, she discovered to her wonderment and delight that her classmates were just like her. "I was in junior high with black girls, brown girls, Asian girls. I was dumbstruck! They were all the same as me!"[3] Ann has said that early experience played a major role in forming her political liberalism years later.

Unfortunately, Roosevelt wasn't a neighborhood school so Ann rarely went to classmates' homes. But she absorbed the diversity of that school so deeply she could never understand racial prejudice afterward.

That was the real difference, for the Texas of Ann's childhood was a wholly segregated state. She had never seen an African American in her community unless it was a man looking for a job as a day laborer or a woman seeking work as a domestic. She later learned that African Americans did live nearby, but only in East Waco, not the better part of town. Also, they had their own all-black school. So there was never any mixing of black and white as there had been in California.

Attending the multicultural Theodore Roosevelt Junior High School was an eye-opening experience for Ann. She always treasured her time there and said that it was instrumental in forming her later political liberalism.

San Diego was the scene of a story Ann once heard and has never forgotten. It involved a woman she would later look up to: Eleanor Roosevelt, wife of President Franklin Delano Roosevelt. When Mrs. Roosevelt visited the naval hospital in San Diego, officials wanted to photograph her there. However, she insisted that they include an African-American man in the picture with her.

The impressionable Ann heard a lot of talk about this incident. Even then she thought that it was an exciting stand and Eleanor Roosevelt a remarkable woman.

Many years later, when she was governor of Texas, a writer asked Ann which women in politics she most admired. Her answer was Eleanor Roosevelt and Barbara Jordan (the first African-American woman from the Deep South elected to the U.S. House of Representatives), but for different reasons. Mrs. Roosevelt "took the side of people who really had no voice in our country," she said. " . . . In race relations . . . [for] the poor . . . basically, she saw the humanity in us all." As for Ms. Jordan, Ann pointed out that "when she held office, her demand for ethical behavior was a beacon for politicians."[4]

Today, many young women might respond resoundingly to such a question: "Ann Richards!"

In 1945 the war ended and Cecil Willis was discharged after twenty-two months in the Navy. Then Ann returned to Texas with her parents.

3

Back Home Again

When she returned to Lakeview, Ann renewed earlier friendships and continued junior high school.

After graduation, the family moved to Waco so Ann could have a "big-town education."[1] Clearly, they recognized what this meant for her future. As she later said, "It must have been after Mamma and Daddy had gone to California that their world opened up, too."[2]

When she enrolled in Waco High, Ann dropped her first name, Dorothy. Classmates would think the combination of names "country," she felt. Since they seemed "big-city" compared to the Lakeview kids she'd known, they had to be more sophisticated. Or so she thought.

In Waco, Ann saw her chance to start life over. And what better place for this than high school, where the name change moved her toward being a "somebody."[3]

Strange as it may appear, for someone who had been reared by loving parents and admired as a child for her winning ways, Ann often felt inferior. She thought she wasn't smart enough . . . or pretty enough. Whenever she succeeded at anything, she felt it was just a fluke.

Since the young Ann Willis didn't think very highly of herself, she thought that before long everyone would find out that she was a fraud, an inferior person.

Here was a chance to prove she was worth something, so people would like her. Ann still sensed that her parents expected great things from her and still had no clue as to what they were. Sharing their hopes, she secretly felt that the standards she'd set for herself were way beyond her. But things would soon change. Ann had a double goal: she wanted both a new sense of self-worth and personal popularity.

Characteristically, she started her quest immediately. On the first day of school, all freshmen went through orientation in study hall. That's where Ann went around introducing herself to everyone she saw, all complete strangers. No one else did this and it must have seemed odd to the other students. Ann even saw an old friend from Lakeview, Regina Garrett—called Rusty because of her red hair—among the freshmen. She approached her with a little laugh: "Hi, I'm Ann Willis." Rusty probably recognized her, but she responded coolly, "How old did you say you are?"[4]

Nothing could have been more devastating to the girl intent on making her mark in this new school.

But there were other opportunities. During her freshman year Ann found a mentor: Mattie Bell Coffield, who taught speech. The class included debate, something Ann took to with enthusiasm. She was always proud of her ability to think logically, and has often said that logic is the key to debate. It also requires verbal skills and good oral expression. Ann always scored well there, too. In addition, Miss Coffield had her students debate both sides of any issue, which was excellent training. Ann had to know her thesis, then defend it logically, whatever side she happened to be on.

Ann found a place where she really excelled. Simple speech, or basic debate, was a piece of cake for her. It came naturally and led to honors in other activities, like competition in extemporaneous speech and declamation. (In the former case, Ann spoke without any preparation—off the cuff. When she declaimed, she spoke dramatically about her subject.) While in Miss Coffield's class, Ann also acted in school plays. So at Waco High, speech class was like a dream come true for Ann. From her earliest school days she had always been able to talk. Now she got good grades for it.

Ann's freshman year was memorable for another reason: it gave her a look into another world. That's when she learned about the "Haves" and the "Have-nots."

In Lakeview, the Willises were just like everyone else, neither rich nor poor. Waco was a different story. It was where Ann realized that her family wasn't well-off compared to some of her classmates.

Not that it mattered to Ann or to her parents. But she now feels Iona liked the idea of her daughter going to a school where she might meet kids who weren't poor. Iona simply didn't want Ann to be as poor as she and Cecil had been.[5]

It's not surprising that Ann still remembers the first cashmere sweaters she owned and buying clothes on sale to be kept for the next appropriate season. Many years later, she told the owner of a women's shoe store, "When I got married, I got to go to [your] store and buy a pair of high heel shoes and pay full price. It was the first time I bought anything and paid full price."[6]

Waco High remains in Ann's memory for another reason. It was the site of her first date. She was fourteen and hadn't had the boy-girl friendships familiar to most girls her age, and she wasn't sure how to act.

Since she had been invited to a special dance, Ann needed a special dress . . . and quickly. There wasn't enough time for Iona to make one, but she knew a woman with a formal that would fit Ann. An aunt loaned Ann her fur coat.

It wasn't appropriate for a fourteen-year-old, but Ann didn't know that. She had more on her mind. Facing what many girls would consider a milestone, their first date, she was tied in knots and absolutely terrified. Unfortunately, she didn't know how to dance. The evening would only get worse.

Her date was hardly more skilled on the dance floor than Ann. Even so, that evening should have been the debut of the new Ann—a young lady who would be poised, likeable, and popular. It was not. When she and her date got in line for punch, Ann's nerves gave out. Suddenly, she threw up on the girl ahead of her, her date, the borrowed dress, and the floor—which didn't open up to swallow her as she devoutly wished it would.

It was small wonder that Ann thought her life was over. But of course it was not. As Ann said later, she had never learned to grow up as a teenager: what to say and how to act. But she has always been what is called a quick study. Before long, she fit in.

Her family didn't belong to the local Fish Pond Country Club, but wealthy school friends would invite Ann to play cards by its swimming pool. Although Ann was convinced that she was too skinny to look good in a bathing suit, she went anyway. There, shaded by a big beach umbrella, they played bridge and canasta.

All school dances were held at the Fish Pond. After she learned how to dance Ann went to most of them. As her social life flowered, she had boyfriends who walked her to class, carried her books, and sometimes held her hand. Still self-conscious, she sometimes wondered if this looked funny and people were laughing at her.[7]

However, Ann was never self-conscious about debating before an audience. In fact, she did so well at the speaker's podium she was chosen to represent Waco High at Girls State. It was quite an honor. Girls State was an annual gathering of girls from every high school in Texas. For a full week each summer, they organized a mock government, ran for office, passed bills, and did all the nitty-gritty things real officeholders do. No wonder Ann found Girls State so exciting. It gave her a peek behind the political scenes.

Not that she or anyone else there had an inkling that the future might find them participating in the real political world. In those days girls, and women, wouldn't have dreamed such dreams. No more than any other minority in the United States, such as African Americans or Hispanics or Asian Americans would have done.

Ann looks back on her Girls State experiences fondly. It was where she worked the room, going around introducing herself to other girls, learning about kids from different parts of the state, including areas she hadn't known existed. It was a wonderful opportunity to meet people with different outlooks and backgrounds.

In her senior year at Waco High, Ann was chosen to participate in Girls Nation. Nothing could have been more exciting for Ann. This gathering was like Girls State but on a larger scale. It featured tours taking delegates from all over the country to the major federal departments, such as State and the Treasury. Delegates also met important government figures, such as Georgia Neese Clark, the treasurer of the United States. Her signature was on all the currency. Ann was very impressed. Clark was the only woman she'd seen who was active in the day-to-day business of government.[8]

Once the entire group went to the White House Rose Garden to shake hands with President Harry S. Truman. It was another exciting event because it included what journalists call a "photo opportunity" or "photo op." Ann still recalls that lovely summer afternoon when they posed for what semed like hordes of photographers.

One of those shots caused a small furor back home in Waco. Published in a local newspaper, it showed Ann seated next to an African-American girl. This led to continuous questions when she returned home. No one asked Ann how she'd felt when she met the president or anything about Girls Nation itself. The only thing people in her hometown seemed to want to know was how in heaven's name did she end up sitting next to an African American? Had it happened very often? And just how many African-American girls participated in Girls Nation, anyway? It's hard to judge whether these reactions were mere curiosity or were tinged with racial prejudice. Ann can't say, but she still shakes her head in wonder over the commotion the photograph caused.

One Waco woman was intrigued by that photo. She was Eleanor Richards, often called "a transplanted Yankee."[9] A graduate of Radcliffe College in Cambridge, Massachusetts, she helped found the Waco League of Women Voters. Now she pointed out the picture to her son, David, and asked him, "Why don't you take out a girl like this?"[10]

It was the kind of question a teenaged boy might resent. Yet, as things worked out, David Richards ended up following his mother's suggestion and enjoying it. When they were both seniors, a mutual friend introduced Ann and David at a local drive-in, the A&W Root Beer Stand.

Although his family was part of Waco's elite, David seemed unaffected by this. He'd gone to prep school in Andover, Massachusetts, for eleventh grade because his mother wanted him to get started toward a good education. He hadn't been back long before Ann met him. They clicked from the start. Ann thought he was special, and just knew David would be very important in her life.[11]

He was handsome, Ann says, and had a great sense of humor. In fact, she couldn't remember knowing a boy as interesting as David. On their first date, they went to a very good Waco restaurant, the Elite Cafe. It contrasted sharply with her rare experiences of eating out with her parents; they usually went to inexpensive places featuring Mexican cooking. At the Elite Cafe Ann followed

Ann poses with her mother, Iona, on her high school graduation day in 1950.

David's lead and ordered fried shrimp, which she liked very much. She also liked being with David.

Within a few months, Ann and David were nearly inseparable. They were in the same grade in school. They went to parties and dances together. And when David walked her to class, Ann didn't care what anyone thought. "We had a really good time together," she reminisces.[12]

They were together on senior prom night when she drank too much for the first time.

If there is such a thing as a turning point in a person's life, for some people it could begin with serious drinking. That may have been the case with Ann Richards. For her, senior prom night 1950 was the start of lots and lots of drinking.

She and David spent most of their weekends at a local roadhouse that sold beer, no questions asked, to them and their friends. Since the legal age for drinking was eighteen, this may have been harmless for most of the others; few people were aware at that time of the seriousness of alcoholism. Clearly, Ann could not have known of the possible effects of heavy drinking.[13]

But senior night 1950 was the start of what would become a problem for Ann years later.[14]

First, though, she and David graduated from Waco High together.

4

Once More Into the Real World

In 1950 college loomed for both Ann and David. His mother, whom Ann calls "Mom El," wasn't satisfied with the education David had received in Waco, so she sent him back to Andover for a post-graduate year. Neither he nor Ann liked this. "We were very much in love," she says.[1] She later suspected Mom El wanted to separate them for their own good. "We were just children," Ann explains.[2]

While David went east, Ann could choose from several colleges offering speech scholarships. She was tempted by a women's college in Missouri. Going away to school seemed exciting, but it also meant leaving home.

Ann's folks didn't want her to go away. The scholarships didn't include living expenses, but if she went to Baylor University in Waco she'd save money by living at home. Ann chose Baylor. She has never regretted it.

When David came home for Christmas break, he refused to return to Andover. His parents worked out a compromise. He could come back if he went to the University of Texas at Austin, driving home weekends to be with Ann.

During the second semester of her freshman year, Ann's parents let her move into a campus dormitory. Except for her experiences with Girls State and Girls Nation, plus occasional sleep-overs at friends' houses, Ann had never been away from home. She took to dorm life right away.

Ann also pledged the Delta Alpha Phi sorority. Her DAP membership made a lasting impression. When it came time for the next class to pledge, members discussed which girls they wanted to have join. Ann was stunned.

As far as she could see, the discussions had very little to do with the pros and cons of membership. On the contrary, Ann learned that acceptance was based more on social status than on popularity or character. Ann wondered how she had been accepted when one member said of a pledge, "Her father's a cop. She's not our type." Another member made the sweeping generalization, "She's just not DAP material." That's when Ann decided she wasn't DAP material either![3]

Ann had never anticipated this kind of meanness. "I just couldn't accept that girls were chosen because of

David transferred to the University of Texas at Austin during Christmas break of his freshman year. He wanted to be closer to Ann, who was studying at Baylor University in Waco. Later, Ann would receive her teaching certificate from the University of Texas.

what their parents did for a living," she said many years later.[4] She couldn't stomach refusing membership because of a girl's background or a parent's occupation. "Somehow I felt it was wrong to be where people were excluded for reasons that were not of their own making." So wrong that then and there she decided never to be part of anything like DAP again.[5]

Baylor was a learning experience for Ann in several ways. She developed a social awareness at the DAP pledge discussions, and she also sprouted the seeds of feminist activism.

Not surprisingly, that burgeoning feminism stemmed from her debating activities. It was supported by Glenn Capp, the head of the speech department and coach of the debating team, who was called "Prof" by most of his students.

The boys' debating team had been invited to compete in the biggest tournament of the year, an all-male contest at Notre Dame. "It was a big deal," Ann says about going to that prestigious institution to debate. "But no plans had been made for the girls' team to take a trip of such grand importance, and I went to Prof and told him it was unfair and wrong."[6]

It did not surprise Ann when Prof agreed with her because he was always logical. What did surprise her was that he did something about it. Around the same time as the Notre Dame tournament, Prof took the girls' team to a debating tournament in Louisiana.

Meanwhile, Ann and David kept seeing each other on weekends. He commuted to Waco for about a year and a half until they decided they didn't want to be apart anymore.

She dropped off the debate team in her junior year. Her scholarship stopped, but Ann didn't care. She no longer wanted to compete because it required road trips that kept her away from David.

They solved this problem at the end of their junior year: David transferred to Baylor and they got married. Ann was nineteen. David was twenty. Today, eyebrows might be raised at such an early marriage. But it was accepted then; most of their friends were married around that age. However, some years later with twenty-twenty hindsight, Ann reflected on that early marriage and said once more that she and David had just been children.[7]

But that would be much later. At the start of their marriage everything was new and exciting. It was fun setting up housekeeping in a small apartment near the Baylor campus. It was fun working in a dress shop to help meet household expenses—for rent, groceries, and so on. It was certainly fun being friends with their neighbors in the next-door apartment, Hoye Jean and Win Biedleman.

The Biedlemans came from East Texas, an area Ann had never seen. Every week they would get their hometown newspaper, the *Overton Express*, which called itself "The Only Newspaper That Gives Two Whoops

37

for Overton, Arp, Leveretts Chapel, and Surrounding Communities." Ann recalls the *Express*'s impassioned editorials and what she has called hot mudslinging. When it came to politics, Hoye Jean and Win shared their paper's passions—and Ann found their outlook simply wonderful.[8] It might have been responsible for the new interest she took in school. Never a serious student until then, in her senior year she found she really liked learning. Suddenly Ann realized there were books she wanted to read, but not enough time to do so. She'd go from class to the dress shop. It sometimes seemed as if there wasn't enough time in the day for everything she wanted to do.[9]

In 1954 Ann and David graduated from Baylor. She had earned a degree in speech, her college major; her minor was political science. David's degree was in history.

The time had come to decide what to do next. Although David had enjoyed his history courses he first considered going into business, which might require further schooling. He and Ann discussed the matter seriously. Eventually they decided that David would go to the University of Texas at Austin to study law. Ann would take graduate level speech and English courses toward a permanent teaching credential.

It was a start toward greater involvement for Ann in the "real world."

5

Wearing Two Hats

After she completed her graduate studies and practice teaching, Ann taught social studies at Fulmore Junior High School in Austin from 1955 until 1957.

"Teaching was the hardest work I had ever done," she has said, "and it remains the hardest work I have done to date."[1] She explains that any serious teacher faced various roadblocks. Parents would complain. Students would complain. Sometimes administrators weren't up to their jobs. Yet, through it all, teachers were expected to pass on knowledge to their students. Ann claims they would be lucky to succeed at this 20 percent of the time.[2]

Difficult though it may have been, Ann enjoyed teaching enormously. She has always relished challenges, and nothing could be more challenging than trying to inspire a class of teenagers. She wanted them to learn and to remember what they had learned. Many of her former students speak warmly of their experiences in Ann's class, so it seems that she succeeded in reaching those goals.

Most of Ann's students came from middle-class homes. Some were children of migrant farm workers and faced various obstacles. First, many couldn't remain in any one school for long. They had to move on when their families headed north in search of new work.

Also, since their families needed the additional money, most of them had jobs after school. They'd leave after the final bell and head for the store they helped to sweep, or the bakery where they washed pans. Home by early evening, they'd eat dinner and later try to do homework before going to bed.

Ann still remembers one such boy. She would look up from her desk and see him half asleep. There was nothing wrong with him, she insists. There were other students like him. These kids who had to work after school simply weren't as quick or alert as those who didn't. They were certainly bright enough, but they were just plain tired.[3]

The seeds of the compassion that Ann later brought to elective office were sown in those Austin classrooms.

In the early years of their marriage, David went to school for his law studies while Ann taught school. At week's end, they always made their way to the Scholz

Beer Garden, an old-fashioned outdoor cafe made for relaxing. Seasoned political actitivists mingled with ordinary customers there, neither group invading the other's turf.

Ann and David usually spent their Friday evenings at the table informally set aside for a bunch that called themselves the Horses Association. They spent hours discussing political issues, picking apart arguments pro and con, and rarely settling anything.

The group had no by-laws, officers, or anything else clubs usually have. To become a Horse Associate you just had to find a seat at the table. In a way those evenings helped prepare Ann for the back-and-forth, give-and-take of political activity. These were raucous, noisy occasions where everyone had something important to toss into the conversation, or at least they thought so.

The mid-fifties were an important period for the Texas Democratic party. Its liberal wing, led by Lyndon B. Johnson, was trying to break the hold of the conservatives, who usually endorsed Republican candidates. Ann and David lined up with the LBJ forces.

As a favor to a friend, David helped the liberal Young Democrats at the University of Texas (UTYD) by distributing flyers on campus. At the first UTYD meeting that he and Ann attended, David was elected president of the group. But there was one problem: He knew nothing about handling a meeting agenda.

Ann has always been concerned with the education and well-being of young people. Former students still speak warmly of Ann's inspirational method of teaching.

Ann did. She had taken a course in parliamentary procedure at Baylor. So she became parliamentarian, the person who keeps order during debates. During most of the UTYD meetings that followed, Ann continued learning about political tactics. The knowledge would come in handy some years later.

When David graduated from law school he was offered a job by a Dallas legal office specializing in labor law. At that time there were very few such firms in the state. Since he liked the idea of working with such a progressive group, he accepted.

Ann learned she was pregnant with their first child. She quit her teaching job and went back to Waco to wait for the big day. Cecile, named for Cecil Willis, was born on July 15, 1957. Six weeks later, they returned to Dallas.

Along with her new maternal responsibilities, Ann kept up with David politically. (He had become a Democratic precinct chairman in Dallas.) In those days, political involvement for women boiled down to carrying out all the tedious chores that they had always done as volunteers: stuffing envelopes, handing out bumper stickers, and the like.

But Ann was still a wife and mother. She sewed clothes for Cecile and herself and as she sums it up: "I cleaned, I cooked, I did what you do [as a homemaker]."[4]

In those years Ann and David developed warm friendships with Sam and Virginia Whitten, and Billie and Andrew Holley. They all shared their dinners and their politics—and included their babies in these activities. The Richardses would cart Cecile over to friends' homes in her carriage and put her to sleep in a back room. Or the others would reverse this procedure and bring their babies to Ann and David's place.

Those evenings were filled with good-natured arguments over the political issues of the day. Sometimes other friends dropped by and joined in. If they lived outside Texas, they'd bring word from that other world. It was exhilerating, with everyone expounding pet views on world problems over sodas and snacks.

The state was rigidly segregated when the Richardses lived in Dallas. Although the U.S. Supreme Court had ruled in 1954 against the "separate but equal" education of the past, Texas was dragging its feet in obeying the court's order to integrate schools "with all deliberate speed," as were other southern states.

Ann was continually outraged by this. She considered it stupid and self-defeating. While she couldn't fight it full time, she did involve herself in activities that didn't interfere with her family responsibilities.[5]

For example, one evening Ann asked David to mind one-year-old Cecile while she went to work in a political campaign. She had just heard a dynamic woman, Juanita Craft, speak of the needs of African-American students and she wanted to help. So she went to the East Dallas headquarters of the National Association for the Advancement of Colored People (NAACP). She stuffed envelopes there for the gubernatorial campaign of Henry Gonzalez.

It was an eye-opener. Gonzalez was Hispanic, as were many of his volunteers. Since it was NAACP headquarters, many African-American volunteers also helped. That's how, in 1958, Ann caught a glimpse of what the Reverend Jesse Jackson later labeled The Rainbow Coalition—people of every color and background working together for political and social justice. It was an exhilerating experience. Ann liked it.

During their third year in Dallas, Ann and David bought a house in what was becoming an integrated neighborhood. David was concerned over the financial commitment that home ownership entailed. But Ann, pregnant with their second child, Dan, thought only of the extra space they would need for their children's growing years.

Ann remembers that house as a happy place filled with people. Young Democrats came from all over for meetings and conventions. Ann and David threw parties, charging a two-dollar admission to cover expenses.

It was an especially demanding time. Ann continued her involvement with political campaigns as well as the civil rights movement. That's when she helped organize the Dallas Committee for Peaceful Integration.

Ann worked in the Dallas headquarters of the Kennedy-Johnson campaign in 1960. She hired a baby-sitter once a week, and again spent days at the menial jobs traditionally handled by women volunteers. They made arrangements for Democratic voters to get rides to the polls, handed out yard signs, or passed out bumper stickers. It was like a replay of the Henry Gonzalez campaign.

But the presidential campaign was different. John F. Kennedy was elected president.

Like many liberal young men at that time, David wanted to join JFK's New Frontier. By then a seasoned civil rights and labor lawyer, he thought he could contribute something on the national level. Someone— no one knows who—agreed, and David became a staff attorney at the Civil Rights Commission. Excitement was in the air as the Richards family packed for Washington.

Ann and David rented a house on Capitol Hill and settled down to enjoy their new experience. Enjoy it Ann certainly did! They were in the nation's capital and she wanted to experience as much of it as possible. In fact, she hired a baby-sitter once a week, then went to the Senate to spend the day in the gallery listening to debates.

Even so, Ann's enjoyment of Washington life lasted only about six months. David became disillusioned with his position and all the bureaucratic hang-ups it involved. Much of their social life consisted of attending cocktail parties where people gossiped about the private lives of those in political power. In addition, now that she had become an activist, Ann wasn't comfortable with having nothing to do.

"We really felt we were kind of useless," Ann said. "I had been living an active political life, and I'm suddenly reduced to making cookies for [Capitol Hill] house tours in Washington."[6]

After a year in the capital, the Richardses packed up again and returned to Dallas, where Ann really began to taste what political activism was all about. But first she had to test herself by leaving it altogether.

6

Ann Wins!

After their return to Dallas, Ann gave birth to her second son, Clark. Soon afterward, she was back in the thick of things. For starters, she and several friends founded the North Dallas Democratic Women (NDDW). As Ann said afterwards, they realized the Democratic party was controlled by men who looked on women as "little more than machine parts." They created the NDDW "to do something substantive."[1]

They went about things systematically. "We kept a card file upstairs in my house," Ann explains. "We were literally trying to get the names of every Democrat on 3x5 cards."[2]

The NDDW also organized the Dallas Committee for Peaceful Integration, something close to Ann's heart. She had long felt that letting white and black children go to the same schools was simply the right thing to do. She wouldn't accept class and racial hatred, especially when it kept children separate.

The Dallas years were a whirlwind of social and political activity for Ann and David. It sometimes seemed as if their home had a revolving door, with people constantly coming through for one reason or another, and often spending the night on a couch in the den.

During that period, Ann also helped the United Farm Workers (UFW). A couple of UFW union organizers came to town and tried to block sales of melons raised on a local nonunion farm. Because she believed in their cause, Ann accompanied them, and dressed in her best, introduced these young people to store managers so they could make their pitch. They didn't meet with much success.

But Ann went about things in her own way. She visited her local supermarket and spoke to the owner. "This is really a serious matter," she told him. "It's serious to the people who harvest those melons" . . . and to Ann, who believed in what they were trying to do.[3] Since she was a valued customer, the owner agreed not to stock the fruit. Thanks to Ann, one store boycotted the melons.

Yet, she says that was minor. Her political activities generally involved making phone calls and stuffing envelopes. Her everyday life mixed children's birthday parties, Scout meetings, and all that went with being a homemaker with a large family. So she juggled the public and the private, enjoying it all enormously. In November 1963 she gave birth to her fourth child, Ellen. It hardly slowed her down.

In 1969, Ann and David decided on a change of scene. After dozens of scouting trips, they found a new house in Austin. It was the home she still remembers as a place that was always filled with people, music, and laughter.[4]

During her first years in Austin, Ann dropped out of political activity. "When I left Dallas, I felt that this was a chance to do something different," she said later. "It was a great opportunity to get out of the rut. I had two children in school. To me that was freedom. I was going to find new directions, discover myself."[5]

Yet Ann took time to help someone who wanted many of the things she did. In 1971 a stranger, Carol Yontz, asked her to lunch with a woman who wanted to run for state office. Sorry, Ann said, she'd left politics behind. She wanted to do other things with her life.[6]

But Yontz was very persuasive. The would-be candidate, Sarah Weddington, needed advice. That name rang a bell. Ann remembered reading about the lawyer who argued the *Roe* v. *Wade* case before the U.S. Supreme Court. In 1973 the Court overturned, by a vote of 7 to 2, state laws prohibiting a woman's right (based on a Constitutional, but not unlimited, "right of personal privacy") to have an abortion within the first three months of pregnancy. The lawyer was Weddington. All right, Ann would meet with Sarah.

The twenty-five-year-old Weddington said that she'd been learning politics was a man's game. "I felt the only way for women to be represented was . . . to learn to run campaigns," she later said. Weddington saw herself as a woman's champion, which might explain why she couldn't find a man with political experience who would help her.[7]

Although she was a babe in the political woods, Weddington had an impressive legislative wish list: She wanted laws that gave women the right to credit in their own names, not their husbands'; laws that made it illegal to fire pregnant teachers; and laws that protected rape victims by focusing on the attacker, instead of on the victim's character.

Weddington wanted a lot, but most of all she hoped to break the tradition that kept women out of the legislature. She would be running against two men.

Ann liked the idea. It was an opportunity to show that governing isn't just men's work. Weddington, the first real feminist Ann had ever met, spoke of the really tough issues women faced. But with no political experience, she needed help organizing her campaign and getting out the vote. Ann could do that. The question was, would she?

It was an invitation Ann could not refuse. Here was an opportunity to wield real authority in a cause she had long supported. While money was always a problem, manpower, or more specifically womanpower, was not. Austin women plunged in on a campaign that was about and for them. It ended with the successful election of Sarah Weddington.

After the election it was back to real life for Ann. But after one legislative session, Weddington asked Ann to come aboard again as her administrative assistant.

For the next two years, Ann managed Weddington's office and learned more about how government activities are organized. Her duties included helping to lay out a legislative package, planning with Weddington what she would do in the session, and hiring staff to track her legislative bills.

Weddington recalls the enthusiasm Ann brought to her job. "Even back then [Ann] was so much more than a housewife. She was involved with her kids, weekend outings, camping. She did everything with gusto."[8]

Political analysts date the beginning of the modern Texas women's movement from the success of Weddington's campaign and its aftermath: trips around the state holding workshops for volunteers. Ann now says, "Some twenty years ago, a little core of Austin women began to organize in a very systematic way to teach women how to negotiate, whether it was in the PTA or the Texas legislature."[9]

Working in Weddington's office—plus the after-hours organizing—was Ann's *job*. Her *life* was with her family. "First and foremost, I was a Mom," she says.

"I learned more about management from running a household than from any other other occupation."[10]

Ann managed to be involved with her children's activities. But she had so many run-ins with her kids' school that she eventually placed them in a private one.

Her older daughter triggered one clash by wearing a black armband on a national day of protest for the Vietnam War. The principal called Ann about it. For discipline's sake, he wanted to send Cecile home.

Always on a short fuse in matters of injustice, Ann blew up. This was a question of free speech, she said.[11] Yet Cecile was making a principled stand on an important issue. Students should be encouraged to follow their conscience on the proper occasion, Ann maintained. A few more incidents like that led to the private school.[12]

Although she regretted leaving the public school system, Ann found it paid off. For one thing, the new school was integrated while public schools were not. When she saw how poorly the local school district prepared children for various future needs, including an integrated society, there was no contest.

With her gift for the colorful phrase, Ann once described her life during those frenetic Austin years as "a tossed salad that's bigger than most bowls."[13]

In 1974 a friend from Weddington's campaign asked Ann for help in an African-American woman's race for the Austin seat in the state legislature. The candidate,

Wilhelmina Delco, shared Ann's views about higher education opportunities for minority students, teenage pregnancy, and other social issues. Ann pitched in, though she later said Delco had been so good she hadn't needed much help. She came up with another winner: Delco became the first African-American woman legislator from Travis County, Austin's base.

Yet again, Ann switched off her public persona, going from campaign work to running her household. But within a year she again donned her public hat. This time it was the beginning of something historic.

In 1973 local Democrats asked David to run in the primary for Travis County commissioner. But he was happy as an attorney and saw no reason to change. Then the party turned to Ann.

David encouraged her to take on this new challenge. But Ann had never wanted to serve in public office. Although Ann had enjoyed all the planning and campaigning, she closed the door on it with relief once her candidates were elected. For Weddington and Delco faced heavy duties that could be overwhelming, while Ann dealt merely with household and family matters.

More to the point, could a woman be elected to this office? It involved what was usually called men's work, or as Ann put it: "a truck-driving, front-end-loader operation, taking care of the roads."[14]

Of course, it's more than that. Texas county commissioners help establish tax rates, oversee the building and maintenance of jails and public buildings. In other words, the job deals with a large infrastructure. Could Ann win this race? Could she do the job?

First she had to study the numbers. This meant going over statistics from a successful campaign run by a city councilwoman in the Travis County area. She and David spent a month going over numbers. Whatever way they looked at it, the numbers said she could win the race. But Ann was troubled by an intuitive sense that her marriage might not survive if she won.[15] Still, David was supportive. He offered to take over management responsibilities of the household and to be Ann's surrogate in delivering the kids to gyms, and dance and piano lessons. She should make this run. If she didn't, she'd always wonder how well she would have done.

Finally convinced of the possibility of success, and intrigued by the challenge of the office, Ann said she would go for it. That decision was the turning point in her life. From then on, her role as wife and mother would take second place to a public career. Instead of serving her family, Ann would give her life to public service.[16]

In 1976 with the help of a solid grassroots organization, Ann beat the three-term incumbent and became the first female commissioner of Travis County.

7

Making it Politically

At first, the men in Ann's office didn't hide their resentment at working for a woman. She handled this potential problem with her usual flair. Early on she gave one crew a pep talk, emphasizing the importance of everyone working together. It fell flat. Thirty men heard her out and when she asked for questions, thirty pairs of eyes just stared at her.

Then Ann had an idea. To break the ice she mentioned an ugly dog she'd seen on her way to the office. "What's its name?" she asked. After a long silence, a man in the back row growled, "Her name is Ann Richards." Instead of being offended, Ann burst out laughing. It was contagious; the whole room quickly exploded with the sound of masculine roars of laughter.[1]

A young man in the front row added hopefully, "But we call her Miz Ann." More laughter followed. From then on, Ann and her crew were a team, and good friends.[2]

"She was a great commissioner," Richard Moya told the *Dallas Morning News* in 1982. Having worked with Ann, he spoke from experience: "[Ann] knew what county government was all about, and she put in time. . . . She helped start an innovative program providing human services and now we fund 39 programs," among them a battered women's center and another for rape victims.[3]

Ann often applied her fertile imagination to other services, such as the Infant Parent Training Program (IPT) for parents of children with Down's syndrome, a form of mental retardation. Research had shown that these children could go to public school with other kids and lead fairly normal lives. But they needed special training, which had to begin very early.

In her first term, Ann learned of planned cuts in the IPT budget. She often says budget-cutting boils down to eliminating funds for a program when people don't see those affected by the cuts. Claiming the IPT was too good to lose, she urged parents of Down's syndrome children to bring their youngsters to Commissioner's Court for the budget hearings. Once the funding staff saw the human faces for whom the money was slated, they wouldn't cut the budget, she said. About twenty families showed up that day, and no cuts were made. The roomful of kids made the difference, Ann felt.

Then there were Travis County's abused children. When Ann heard the court planned to scale back on protective services for battered kids, she had her staff collect photos showing what they look like. "Abuse" is just a word until you see what happens when there's not enough money to take these youngsters away from an environment where they're mistreated. "You can't sleep with that," Ann said.[4] She didn't, and the photographs helped to save the program's budget. It is no wonder that Ann gained a reputation as an enormously popular and efficient administrator.[5]

Being commissioner took all of Ann's time and energy. She says officeholders don't have ordinary work days. Her calendar could include appearances at local charities, neighborhood committee meetings, or service clubs at any hour of the day—or night. Her working hours were not the usual nine to five.

During those years, Ann grew as a feminist. In 1977 she attended the International Women's Year Convention in Houston. Delegates hoped to work out a statement of principle on women's issues. With passage of the Equal Rights Amendment high on their agenda, many delegates wanted a strong statement supporting the ERA in their platform.

When they lined up at the microphones to speak, former Congresswoman Bella Abzug, the conference chair, saw Ann and called, "Come on, Texas."[6]

Ann spoke eloquently for ". . . the voiceless, the divorced woman who may not be able to get credit, the widows . . . incapable of earning a living . . . my own daughter who cannot find women in [her] textbooks . . ."[7]

The Houston convention became a landmark in Ann's life as she began to network with women from around the country. Soon invitations to similar events poured in.

For such occasions she devised a comic figure, "Harry Porko," to personify sexism in the business world. With a pig rubber mask and exaggerated drawl, Ann played Harry, the male-chauvinist boss. "I take good care of my girls," Ann/Harry said with a wink. Anyone with a faultless attendance record got a plastic yellow rose for her uniform. "Women appreciate things like that," she/he added. "My girls are happy because I know how to treat 'em. A smile of appreciation, a pat, that means more to a girl than any amount of money."[8] Ann expanded Harry for political roasts across the country, always drawing hysterical laughter from female audiences.

Those activities occurred "after hours." During the day, Ann remained a public official. Sitting on the commissioner's court brought new independence. Ann made decisions on matters affecting people's lives—for example, how to spend their tax money—and she did so without consulting David. "That was no small thing," she has said.[9]

Other feminist issues arose for Ann. In one case, she responded as both a public figure *and* a mother. It happened after a visit to the Texas Institute of Cultures in San Antonio. Along with collections of state artifacts, the institute features a slide show telling visitors all about the state. As the family left the auditorium, her daughter, Ellen, then seven or eight, pulled at Ann's sleeve. "Where were all the women?" she asked.[10]

Ann was stunned. How could she have missed this major hole in the story they had just seen? For she now realized that there were only two women in the slide show, and one was an English actress![11]

When they returned home, Ann considered Ellen's question. How could her daughters understand who they were and where they had come from if they didn't feel their own history? Then she swung into action, determined to change things. She began at the Texas Foundation for Women's Resources. Its board of directors included Ann, her administrative assistant, Jane Hickie, and Mary Beth Rogers, a communications consultant long active in state politics. Ann told them there was no history of women in Texas and they agreed that something had to be done.

Four years later, they completed a project that was literally started from scratch. Until then, there had been *no* history of Texan women. The group oversaw fresh research in just about every area: business, culture, and personal histories. It was a lot of work, but the results were gratifying. After its completion, Ann and the board decided this archive should become a traveling exhibit, set up in various public sites across the state where people could see it.

Around then, the National Women's Political Caucus decided to get more women involved in politics. Ann and Rogers adapted tactics from the county commissioner's race to work for *any* political campaign. Further, they reached women who had little interest in politics but who needed to learn techniques that would lead to success in PTAs, in community groups, and before municipal councils. They also taught these women how to raise funds for their goals.

Ann and her team gave "how-to" seminars wherever they were invited to speak, always keeping their message simple. They might emphasize body language—for example, crossed arms in front of your chest is a defiant pose. Sit back in your chair to show you're in command. When you're on television, smile! People in your home audience will smile back automatically and be more willing to accept your message.

Over those years, Ann continued working very hard as county commissioner. It was during this time that she realized her marriage was disintegrating. This led her to drink—a lot.

Ann would be the first to say that her crumbling marriage didn't cause a growing dependence on alcohol.[12] But she says that she thought the pain of living was lessened when she drank. Ann eased that pain most days by drinking with colleagues after work at a nearby bar.[13]

This habit began to trouble Ann. Eventually, she confided her worries to a doctor. It didn't help. When she told him she drank from three to four martinis a night, he reassured her that it was nothing to worry about. He drank that much himself.[14]

His answer didn't help. Ann now knows alcoholism is a biological, pyschological disease that must be fought head-on.[15] This is the thinking behind most programs that help treat the problem.

Fear was partly the reason Ann drank. She had begun to see that the only thing that mattered, her marriage, was failing. During that traumatic time she thought she would die if she were no longer married to David. It was devastating to recognize that this was no longer possible. They had grown too far apart to mend matters.[16]

Like many professionals, in the later years of their marriage they had begun to follow different paths. When Ann made out-of-town speeches, she asked David if he wanted to come, but understood when he didn't.[17] Increasingly he passed on her invitations. So she had to deal with her problem more or less by herself.

Ann's recovery from alcoholism began when Jane Hickie noticed her downhill slide. Hickie had learned about John and Pat O'Neill, who taught families how to intervene in an alcoholic's life. When Hickie told them about Ann they agreed to help.

One Sunday morning in January 1980, Sue Sharlot, a longtime friend, dropped in on Ann. She said that she was concerned about her father. He had had an accident. Would Ann come to her house and keep her company? Sure, Ann said, as soon as she got dressed. Half an hour later, she walked into Sharlot's living room and got the shock of her life. Sharlot wasn't alone. She and her husband, Michael, together with David, Dan and Cecile (their two older children), and some of Ann's best friends sat facing the door—and her. There were also two strangers whom she soon learned were the O'Neills. "I was terribly frightened," Ann said.[18]

When she caught her breath, John O'Neill invited Ann to sit down. He said, "Your friends are very concerned about you." On this cue everyone made a brief, to-the-point statement. They described things Ann had done, concluding by saying, "I know you would not have done that if you hadn't been drinking."[19] Ann couldn't miss the connection. She listened in a kind of fog.

Afterward, a heavy silence hung over the room. Nearly everyone was crying, especially Ann. Then John O'Neill spoke. "You have a disease," he told her, "and everyone wants you to get treatment. There is help," he concluded.[20]

Ann's strong family ties have helped her through grueling times in her life—most especially, her battle against alcoholism. Pictured here at Christmastime are: (left to right) Dan Richards; Ann Richards; Cecile Richards, holding son Daniel; Kirk Adams (Cecile's husband), holding daughter Hannah; Ellen Richards; Clark Richards; (front row, left to right) Lily Adams; Iona Willis; Cecil Willis.

"I felt a great wash of relief that perhaps there was some way out for me," Ann says. "Where is that help?" she asked.[21]

The best place was St. Mary's Hospital in Minneapolis, O'Neill said. She could leave that afternoon. They had an airline ticket in her name.

Ann went home to pack. As she did so, a new fear arose. Once word got out, it would mean the end of her political career. How could it be otherwise? After all, she was a public figure who should be above reproach.[22]

Still, Ann signed into St. Mary's. She attended numerous group therapy sessions, heard speakers from Alcoholics Anonymous (AA) and received private counseling. The treatment lasted a month.

Yet, when she first returned home, Ann couldn't rid herself of new fears. Had the program destroyed her sense of humor? Her natural zaniness? Not at all, she soon found. And by shedding her self-destructive behaviour, Ann gained a new appreciation for living in every sense.

After her return, Ann met with the friends who had intervened for her. She wasn't cured, she said. Recovery is a lifetime process. But she'd keep working at it, she told them. And she would succeed.[23]

Then talk turned to political matters. Her friends advised her very firmly to keep mum about where she'd been the previous month.

After neatly closing the book on her month at St. Mary's, Ann still had to consider her marriage. She recognized that she and David no longer followed the same paths. Their lives had changed radically since she'd become county commissioner and they were completely different people from the young couple who had married over thirty years earlier.

But Ann and David didn't give up easily. They worked with a marriage counselor, but it didn't help. They separated a few years before their final, amicable divorce was granted in 1984—well over thirty years after they had married.

"Getting a divorce was . . . the most difficult and sad thing that ever happened in my life," Ann says.[24]

Now alone, Ann took the lessons she'd learned at St. Mary's back to her post as county commissioner. She continued doing a superior job. In fact when the time came, she easily won reelection. Then she went on to further political triumphs.

8

Catching the Public Eye

Not long after the divorce, Ann spoke of her new solitary life. It was "terribly difficult" to adjust to living alone, she said. "But I learned how to do it . . . now I love the quiet and don't get lonely."[1]

Now it never could be said that Ann Richards's life has been simple. There were many times when a bombshell would go off, so to speak. This happened in January 1982 when she got a call from an old friend, Bob Armstrong, then a candidate for governor. Armstrong said the incumbent state treasurer and much of his staff had been subpoenaed to testify before a grand jury.

"That's interesting," Ann said. "But what's it to me?"[2] Then Armstrong threw the bombshell. Since things looked bad for Treasurer Warren Harding, the

Democratic party needed someone to run for his office. Ann was that someone.

"But I don't know a thing about being state treasurer," Ann protested, "you're crazy!" Then he said "You can do it, it's time for a woman to be on the ticket, and you're the only who gives us real hope."[3]

No way could she do it, Ann said. There were lots of reasons why this was out of the question. She was about a year out of the St. Mary's program, separated from David, a woman living alone. Politically, she'd be extremely vulnerable on any of those counts.[4]

Still, Armstrong kept trying to talk Ann into running, appealing to her party loyalty as well as to her feminism. All right, Ann said, she'd think about it.

For most of that day, Ann's phone almost rang off the hook. Friends called, urging her to take on this challenge. Liz Carpenter, former press secretary to President Lyndon B. Johnson's wife, Lady Bird, scoffed when Ann said she didn't know if she could do the job. "Oh, Ann, you can do anything," Carpenter said. "Don't worry about that."[5]

Later that day Ann spoke again with her friends. They all agreed she should have a shot at the race. "It turned out that I had unintentionally built a base with my speaking trips," Ann says, "people thought I could do the job and, frankly, help the Democratic party."[6]

By evening, Ann said that if they could raise

Richards learned to field questions from the press after she announced her decision to run for the office of state treasurer.

$200,000 in pledges for her campaign in the next twenty-four hours, she'd go for it. Meeting her challenge, they burned up the phone lines, and raised the money well within her deadline.

Always known for her meticulous organizational skills, Ann threw herself into the preparations. She called an old friend, Suzanne Coleman. "Just what does a state treasurer do?" she asked. Could Coleman do some fast research on this and report the results back quickly?[7] No sooner asked than answered. The following day, Coleman gave Ann a step-by-step briefing. Other friends began to research information they thought useful and passed it on.

The next day, Ann hopped on a plane with that data and made a nine-city tour of Texas announcing her candidacy at each stop, spelling out the changes she would make in the office. Ann has always been a good saleswoman. She sold herself on that tour, detailing those changes.

It was just the beginning. Ann had to plan two campaigns: one for the May primary, and one for the November general election. Further, she had to start at once from ground zero. For instance, she had lists of likely supporters, but no computer to match them with specific issues. Most important, though, she had volunteers. As Ann said later, "People were coming out of the woodwork to help."[8] That enthusiasm mixed with sleeves-rolled-up, energetic, old-fashioned politicking became a powerful force.

Ann also needed someone to travel with her while she covered the largest of the lower forty-eight states. Someone dependable, like her older son Dan, who was then twenty-two years old. She told him, " . . . I need a man to travel with me. . . . Are you willing to give me the next nine months of your life?" He didn't hesitate. "Yes," Dan said, and immediately became essential to the campaign *and* to Ann.[9]

(Ann's other children were old enough to take care of themselves. For instance, Cecile was working as a union organizer.)

It was a close collaboration. Dan kept them to tight schedules, sometimes acting as Ann's advance man, reminding her of people she had to see. All in all, it was a full day's job, week after week. They'd start around six in the morning and get to sleep around midnight, eating at odd hours if they hadn't attended a meeting that included some kind of meal.

As is true of any modern political campaign, money was its life's blood, so Ann also had to raise funds for the race.[10] This aspect of politics hadn't changed. If anything, campaigns were becoming even more expensive. The race for treasurer cost $1 million.

It wasn't easy work. Mother and son set off on itineraries covering a series of towns a week at a time. Whenever possible, some supporter would set up an "event" where Ann could meet local people whose views counted. Or she would go to a local newspaper trying to get some kind of coverage, either a news story or an editorial. If the town had a radio station she would organize a press conference—so much the better if it had a television outlet that also could help spread her story. When none of the local media came, Ann went to them, trying to get onto a newscast.

Obviously, this type of campaigning can be grueling. At one point, Ann called Cecile, then organizing in New Orleans. "I really need you," she told her daughter.[11] That was enough. Cecile took a leave of absence and went north for her assignment. Setting off by car, she stayed in private homes to save money. Hitting town after town, she managed very well indeed. Ann proudly recalls an editorial endorsement in a town she'd never heard of thanks to her daughter.[12] At another point, Dan and Cecile traveled together going to local radio stations for interviews.

About a month into the campaign Lane Denton, once Ann's friend, threw his own bombshell. Also competing for party endorsement in the primary, he staged a press conference in Austin revealing that Ann was an alcoholic who had been treated for her problem. And, he said, she'd been under treatment for a mental disorder. A former colleague on the county court, David Samuelson, wrapped up this underhanded hatchet job.

One of Ann's favorite breaks from the hectic pace of her life is to spend time with her grandchildren. Here she is enjoying the aquatic sights at the San Antonio Sea World with granddaughter Lily.

She had been a poor commissioner, he said. There was really something wrong with Ann.[13]

It's easy to picture how these reports affected Ann's campaign. The media wanted answers to the charges, and she had to speak with *every* caller. Yes, Ann said, she was an alcoholic. But she had received treatment, was in recovery, and was very positive about everything,

That hardly helped. Denton had Ann's itinerary for each town. So wherever she stopped, her drinking and treatment were hashed over and over in newspaper articles and on radio programs. The media paid little attention to campaign issues. They only asked Ann about her drinking.

She knew how to answer. Thanks to her St. Mary's treatment, she was prepared for this. Yet, while Ann knew she'd survive such attacks, she was saddened at having to respond publicly to a private matter.

The primary eliminated Lane Denton and another contender, leaving Ann and Warren Harding in the run-off for the general election. Within a few days, though, Harding dropped out. Ann and her staff greeted this news gleefully. If they had gone through the run-off, it would have cost an additional two or three hundred thousand dollars—that they didn't have.

As the Democratic candidate for treasurer, Ann ran against Allen Clark, a Republican with some banking experience. A Green Beret veteran of the Vietnam War, he campaigned largely on the basis of his war record.

On the other hand, Ann now carried a feminist banner in the race; no woman had won a statewide election in fifty years. Hoping to break that string, she campaigned very hard everywhere.

She worked town squares or went from store to store, simply talking to people, most of whom were enthusiastic. They weren't alone. Once, state controller John Sharp introduced Ann to some skeptical Texas midland oilmen. At one point he left the room; when he came back, there was Ann down on her knees shooting dice surrounded by a group of new admirers.[14]

But it was her straight-from-the-shoulder politicking, generously mixed with wit and down-home wisdom, that carried the day. At campaign's end everything paid off. Ann racked up 61.4 percent of the vote.

Now many people might feel a state treasurer needs a solid background in economics. She or he should be good with figures and know how to handle finances. Although Ann hadn't done especially well in school math courses, she could delegate responsibility to people who knew the financial ropes. She did so, building a staff who performed marvelously under her direction.

She called them "a working example of blacks and Hispanics and women, [and] Anglo men, working together and doing a superb job."[15] When Ann took office, 86 percent of the staff was male. After she restructured the agency to reflect state demographics, it became 57 percent white, 13 percent black, 28 percent

Hispanic, and 60 percent female. Half the managers were now female.[16]

Of course, Ann did a great job leading them. That's how she caught the attention of National Democratic Party leaders. They chose her to second the presidential nomination for [then] Vice President Walter Mondale, and she entered the national spotlight by eloquently doing so. Texans knew how good Ann was on the election stump; now the rest of the country got a taste of her witty, down-home style. They liked it.

Meanwhile, Ann energetically carried on as Texas State Treasurer. She personally drew in investments from sources outside the state, including nationally known New York banks. Indeed, she was incredibly successful at earning money for the state—$2 billion in actual fact.[17]

Texas voters approved of Ann's work: with no opposition, she was reelected treasurer in 1988. It was another "first." She is the only woman in state history to serve two consecutive terms. Even before this record, she already had been inducted into the Texas Women's Hall of Fame.

Ten-year-old Kori Clark had also been following Ann's political career. As a fourth-grader she did a paper on "A Texas Woman of History." Choosing Ann as her subject, Kori based the report on information from Ann's office—and concluded with the remark, "I do believe this report was written by a future governor of Texas."[18]

Richards delivered a memorable keynote address at the 1992 Democratic Party National Convention underneath a giant television image of herself with granddaughter Lily.

The teacher who graded Kori's paper commented that she shouldn't set her sights so high for herself since she was a girl. That was too much for Kori, and she wrote to Ann with the whole story.

Kori picked the right role model. "Ann told me I can do whatever I set out to do if I really work at it. And," she added happily, "Ann invited me and my Mom to Austin for a weekend."[19]

It was a memorable experience. Ann showed Kori and Mrs. Clark around the Treasury and other Austin sights. At their visit's end, Ann told Kori that she was thinking of running for governor. "If I win, you can have a slumber party in the Governor's Mansion,"[20] she said.

No wonder Kori calls Ann "just a *great* person," adding, "I just love her to death!" (Like most members of her staff, Kori is on first-name terms with Ann.)[21]

However, before the gubernatorial race, Ann returned to the Democratic Party National Convention in Atlanta—as keynote speaker. It was there, in 1988, that she made her memorable remark about [then] Vice President George Bush having a silver foot in his mouth.

That appearance was a prelude to the crowning achievement of Ann's career—so far. In 1990, she won the gubernatorial race after a bruising battle against a millionaire with no political experience—just the desire to become governor.

9

Madame Governor!

Although Ann was no stranger to down-and-dirty politics, her run for governor would have taken first prize. As George Shipley, who did negative research for her, put it: "The primary . . . was probably the most brutal in the country . . . a regular Texas brawl."[1] And everything went downhill from there. Often trailing her opponent by as many as thirty points, Ann won the general election by one hundred thousand votes out of considerably more than three million cast. It was a real come-from-behind victory!

It all began in June 1988 when Ann wrote to longtime supporters that she was considering entering the toughest political campaign of her career—for governor of Texas. That was all most of them needed. Two women who had long been close to her in the political arena, Jane

Hickie and Mary Beth Rogers, started preparing for action.

As administrative assistant on the Travis County Commission, Hickie had managed Ann's first campaign for treasurer. She also had helped to steer Ann away from alcohol.

Rogers had been deputy treasurer. Always Ann's equal as an organizer, Rogers managed the general campaign when they couldn't find a man to do it their way. Completely unflappable, she directed the troops.

Ann's announcement drew a response from the network of women activists she had inadvertently formed when she showed them how to organize. Now they were eager to pitch in and support her all the way to the voting booth.

Most important of all, the Richards children stood behind their mother, doing an extraordinary job that money never could have bought.

Repeating his role from the campaign for treasurer, Dan gave Ann another nine months of stabilizing support. Daughters Cecile and Ellen rode in parades, raised money, endlessly shook hands, and told everyone how and why their mother would be a great governor. (Ellen took a year off from college for the campaign; Clark, a drug and alcohol counselor, was not as involved in the campaign.)[2]

Cecile's husband, Kirk Adams, was campaign field director, a vital position. With extensive experience as a union organizer, he was a natural for the job. Field workers usually manage phone banks, knock on neighborhood doors, distribute leaflets, and, most essential, get out the vote on election day.

Ann kicked things off in the fall of 1989 at the Women's National Democratic Club in Washington, D.C., where an enthusiastic audience gave generously to her campaign fund. Additional appearances followed in major Texas cities at $1,000-a-plate dinners. By Christmas of that year, more than eleven thousand contributors had signed on for Ann. And she hadn't even officially entered the race.

Six months later she did, declaring, "When I'm governor, one of the things you won't hear is, 'That's not my job!'" She called for "a new Texas" where children would "learn to think and develop their full human capacity in good schools and caring families," and where "drug dealers are punished and treatment is available to all."[3]

Money was as important to this campaign as to every previous one—only more so. It became one of the most expensive in American electoral history, costing over $31 million. Ann's opponent in the general election, political newcomer Clayton Williams, spent $30 million, nearly half of it his own money. Part of Ann's $11 million came from small contributors, her grassroots support.[4]

Political analysts consider name recognition as important as funding. By 1990 many Texans knew about the attractive woman with the silver hair who

In addition to being Ann's son-in-law, Kirk Adams was invaluable to her as field director of her compaign for governer. Adams (center) joined his mother-in-law, the new governor of Texas, in welcoming Jesse Jackson to the Lone Star state.

reduced audiences to helpless laughter with good ol' boy Harry Porko and his sexist remarks. After her 1988 "silver foot in his mouth" keynote address, Ann had *national* recognition.

So when she announced her entry into the gubernatorial race, money began pouring in from all over—especially from outside Texas . . . *lots of money.*

"PAC" is an abbreviation for "Political Action Committee." PACs raise money for candidates that the committee supports, and most of Ann's out-of-state funds came from a PAC called EMILY's list. EMILY is an acronym (a word made up from the first letters of several words) for Early Money Is Like Yeast, it makes the dough rise.

Moving right along, Ann named Barbara Jordan and Henry Cisneros her campaign cochairs. Ann had long admired Jordan, the former African-American congresswoman, who had been a keynote speaker at the 1984 Democratic National Convention. Known for her splendid oratory and gift for zeroing in on civil rights issues, Jordan's support was crucial.

That was also true of Cisneros, a former mayor of San Antonio, who became U.S. Secretary of Housing and Urban Development. In the Hispanic community, Latinos often followed his progressive lead. Cisneros and Jordan were essential members of Ann's team in the general election.

Again, Ann ran two campaigns. In the primary, she faced Mark White and Jim Mattox. White, a former governor, was a moderate Democrat. Mattox was a very popular state attorney general.

The media cited Mattox's superior record on women's issues and the rights of labor and consumers. Yet he could not get endorsements from any of those groups; early polls showed Ann leading him by more than three to one. It must have been frustrating for someone who wanted to become governor very badly.

Perhaps that explains his negative campaigning. For Mattox conducted what many considered one of the ugliest primaries ever. He began with a series of personal smears and continued in that vein. For example, he continually referred to Ann's former alcoholism. Could voters expect an alcoholic "in recovery" to remain that way under the strains of office, he asked over and over.[5]

During an early debate, Mattox also confronted Ann with the question that would be repeated incessantly: Had she ever done drugs? She replied that she hadn't used any mind-altering substance for the previous ten years. It wasn't enough; Mattox demanded a fuller answer. Soon, "Answer the question" could be heard at nearly every press conference. At one point, Ann retorted in no uncertain terms: "I've been sober for ten years. Have Mark White and Jim Mattox been honest for ten years?"[6]

Finally, she said, "I have revealed more about my personal life, including my alcoholism, than [any gubernatorial candidate] and now, by continuing to raise

Although her children are grown-up, Richards now enjoys playing with grandchildren Lily and Dan.

these questions I think we are sending a very strong message to a lot of people who think that if they seek treatment they will forever bear the stigma of their addiction."[7] That was her final word on the subject. She would not elaborate. It was the kind of dignity that impressed many people, especially voters.

The attacks eventually backfired. Neither Denton in the primary for treasurer, nor Ann's opponents in the gubernatorial campaign, convinced people that a former alcoholic couldn't be trusted. Moreover, everyone knew all they wanted to about drugs; they wouldn't let veiled accusations influence their votes. At one of her last press conferences, Ann repeated that she hadn't taken as much as an aspirin for the last decade. "Ten years is a lifetime to me," she declared.[8]

Now Ann took off her gloves and began to give as good as she got. In the words of the *Dallas Morning News*, she came out slugging. First, how could White become wealthy on a gubernatorial salary of $55,000? The year after leaving office, he bought a home worth over $1 million. Why had Mattox accepted $20,000 in campaign contributions from a real estate developer linked to savings and loan fraud? These men had lined their pockets while in public service, and *they* wanted to become governor.[9] White tried to defend himself, Mattox kept charging Ann with drug abuse. Neither tactic worked.

Ann had shown how she could handle the heavy pressures of office. She surged ahead, eliminating Mark White, then pulling out what many called an incredible win over Mattox. According to some analysts, Ann won the gold after convincing voters that Mattox was a bully. The day after the primary, one newspaper headline read that Ann had won in a mudslide—a play on the more familiar "landslide victory."[10]

Ann didn't rest on the laurels of that success. She couldn't. In the general election she had to face a man who wanted to be governor every bit as much as Jim Mattox had. And Clayton Williams could well afford to indulge his ambition. Nor did he hesitate to stoop as low as Mattox had when attacking Ann: coarse sexist remarks; the admission that he hadn't paid income taxes in 1986 because it had been "a bad year" for him; his refusal to shake hands with Ann before a televised debate.[11] Enough voters became convinced that Williams was not the right person to deal with the pressing problems facing their state. He was too clownish, too arrogant.

Williams didn't do himself in alone. As the campaign wound down, Barbara Jordan took Ann to African-American churches seeking support. In the final week she called a press conference and declared in rich, resounding tones that any member of a minority who voted for Williams was out of his or her mind.[12]

Henry Cisneros escorted Ann through various barrios. He made a Spanish-language television spot for her that was broadcast in Hispanic communities, pointing out that turning one's back on a lady is "very ungentlemanly."[13]

Whenever Williams goofed, Ann jumped in to turn things to her advantage. On the radio, she declared: "Millions of average Texans paid taxes . . . while [Williams] took advantage of loopholes for the rich."[14]

Exit polls showed that many Republicans voted for Ann. Overall, 60 percent of women supported her. They made the difference in the end.

On election night, November 6, 1990, Ann attended her Tuesday night AA group as usual. "My name is Ann. I am an alcoholic," she said, then left for the Austin Hyatt-Regency Hotel and a ballroom filled wall-to-wall with her people. Above their heads a big sign proclaimed, "Ann Richards is head of the class."[15]

What some had considered "The Impossible Dream" had actually occurred. Ann was governor-elect! The second woman to be governor in state history and the first to do so in her own right. On entering the room, she unfurled a T-shirt that read: "A Woman's Place Is In The Dome," flashing it to every corner—and setting off pandemonium.[16]

"It looks like the people of Texas are back," Ann remarked happily.[17] When the noise died down, she climbed the podium to address the troops. Her voice almost gone, she thanked everyone for their never-say-die support and their endless energy. In response, the place exploded with cheers and whistles, as Ann and her family left for a much-needed rest.

The following day, about fifty staff members returned for a final wrap-up. Again, Ann thanked those who had contributed to her victory. In her inimitable way she joked and turned serious by turns. "The truth of the matter is that we . . . won this race because of you, not me," she said. "We were part of the whole." She stepped back and added, "I know how I got here." A pause, then she repeated, "*I know how I got here.* And you dance with them that brung you!"[18]

For a while after Ann's earnest, heartfelt thanks, there was hardly a dry eye in the room. (Dan and Ellen Richards sat on the floor weeping together.) A hush came over the room until Ann said, "It's been hard . . . but I think none of us would have traded it for anything. I love you all." Flashing her 1000-watt grin, she reached into a box behind her to triumphantly pull out a shiny blue file folder with the words "Ann Richards Governor" in dark blue letters on the back. Pandemonium resumed.[19]

When the noise died down, Ann invited everyone to accompany her on inaugural day. "We are all gonna gather on the Congress Avenue bridge, and we're going to take back the Capitol for the people of Texas!" she announced in her familiar drawl. And set off one final roar.[20]

10

Ann Gets to Work

At 10:00 A.M. on January 15, 1991, Ann led a crowd of about twenty thousand, their arms linked, up Congress Avenue to the Capitol. She had begun to fulfill her pledge to retake government for the people of Texas.

It was just the start. By the end of ninety days in office, Ann had made over four hundred appointments to state boards and commissions. Of these appointments, 49 percent were women, 21 percent were African-American, 25 percent were Hispanic and 2 percent Asian. Her appointments more closely reflected the state's demographics of 24 percent Hispanic and 12 percent African-American citizens. More importantly, she named more of them to high executive office than any other Texas governor.[1]

During the race, Ann promised to toughen ethical standards for state legislators. To show she meant it, she named Barbara Jordan her special counsel on ethics.[2]

Her high spirits lit up those early days. Once, when Ann saw a familiar face among visitors, she flashed her brilliant smile. "Isn't it great I'm here," she said.[3]

Indeed it was—for Texas. State Representative Steven R. Dolens, of Dallas, has long admired Ann's no-nonsense, straight-from-the-shoulder managerial style. "She's not only hands-on, she gets her hands dirty . . . no governor has done that in a long time and that's why she was able to set the agenda," he said.[4]

On the campaign trail, Ann had promised to make government accessible and efficient. Like a Texas tornado, she cleared away the dead wood as she streamlined state departments. To help make these changes work, she started training programs for hundreds of state agencies.

During her first *week* in office, Ann personally led a surprise midnight raid on a filthy nursing home, dramatizing the sloppy regulation of such facilities.[5]

During her first *month* in office, Ann received more mail than the previous governor got in a year![6]

By the end of her first *year* in office, she had chalked up a winning record of making government "inclusive rather than exclusive, bringing in men and women from all walks of life and viewpoints." As for economic development, she helped attract thirty-one major companies to Texas, providing new jobs where they were needed. Her administration also sent $2.5 million to San Antonio for a special adult job training program.[7]

Ever since her years as a teacher, Ann has stressed the importance of education and she means it. During her first year in office she established a school-to-work transition program that prepares graduating students for the job market or college.[8]

Twelve months after Ann won the gubernatorial race, *The New York Times* applauded her for "practicing the art of the politically possible."[9] She did so by appointing administrators who carried out her campaign promises—such as the Education Commissioner who cut through red tape to restore funds for schools, teachers, and children.

Not long after taking office, Ann kept a special promise—Kori Clark's slumber party. The elegant Governor's Mansion probably hadn't hosted a social event like it before. Festivities included take-out pizza, which had to be ordered twice: someone who answered the pizzeria phone the first time thought it was a prank. After their meal, Kori, ten friends, Ann, her granddaughter Lily, and two bodyguards saw a favorite film at a local theatre.[10]

Later that evening, Ann led a tour of the mansion. The kids stayed over, sleeping in two of its rooms. One was the Sam Houston bedroom. Ann told them, with a twinkle in her eye, that it was supposed to be haunted.

One of Ann's first actions as governor was to keep a special promise—one made to a little girl who had believed in Ann's political future from the beginning. Here, Kori Clark tells reporters about her awesome slumber party at the governor's mansion.

Kori reports with relish that the boys didn't want to sleep there. She and a friend did instead. Today, when speaking of that unforgettable weekend, Kori grins and says, "It was a blast!"[11]

It would be nice to end the Ann Richards story with another win at the polls. But that was not to be.

Ann ran for reelection against George W. Bush, the oldest son of the former president. She lost the race. The final tally was 2,014,399 for Ann vs. Bush's 2,350,493—with only 57 percent of the women's vote going to her.[12]

In an article titled "Bushwacked," Molly Ivins wrote, "Ann Richards was dragged out of office by the fact that 63 percent of the people in this state disapprove of [President] Bill Clinton, and of that 63 percent, most of them can't stand him."[13]

A well-known humorist and political columnist for the *Fort Worth Star-Telegram*, Ivins echoed the views of other electoral analysts. Simply put, they said that voters were in an angry, throw-the-bums-out mood. Even when an office-holder was relatively popular—and Ann was *very* popular—that wasn't enough.

The Economist, a highly regarded British news magazine, noted that Ann had been "the most successful governor of America's second-biggest state in years."[14] She helped push through insurance reforms, strong environmental measures, and a tough government-ethics law—as she had promised four years earlier.

Yet, while nearly two-thirds of Texas voters spoke favorably of Ann in public-opinion surveys, nearly as many voted for Bush. "The biggest factor that [hurt] Ann Richards [was] the political environment. People are . . . angry with politicians," said Mark Sanders, an Austin consultant who worked for Republicans. "The electorate is out hunting for incumbents right now," he said a month before Texans proved it at the polls.[15]

Ann showed her own awareness of this at a convention of conservation officials around that time. Following a long-winded administrator from the U.S. Department of Agriculture, she delivered one of her famous one-liners. "After the USDA's been up here talking to you," she said with that one-and-only grin, "I hesitate to say that I'm from the government and I'm here to help." As ever, she brought down the house.[16]

According to many observers, Ann spent too much time in her reelection campaign comparing her opponent's inexperience to her record as governor; she devoted far less time to putting forth her plans for a second term. On the other hand, she told African-American congregations repeatedly she had remained true to her long-held desire to change the faces in history book illustrations.

Ann was satisfied with having added the faces of minority Texans whom she put in power. "I want the children of Texas to open the history books in their schools and see pictures of people who look like them,"

Governor Richards waves to the downtown Austin crowd during the Desert Storm Heroes Parade.

she said. "And they can say, 'If they can do it, I can do it, too.'"[17]

Ann's face also belongs in those books. Lisa McMinn, a young Austin lawyer, unwittingly confirmed this when she reminisced about having seen Ann at [University of Texas] Lady Longhorns basketball games. ". . . I would watch all the kids come up and shake her hand," McMinn said, "and how much the little girls looked up to her."[18]

Regardless of election results, many people still look up to Ann. She appreciates it. In a "Dear Friend" post-election letter to supporters, she wrote, "Well, it didn't turn out the way we planned. But, life rarely does. And, as I said on election night, this is the end of a campaign, not the end of the world."[19]

Ann went on to express pride in "all we've accomplished over the past four years . . . [having] made a deep impression on Texas—one that the results of an election can never erase." She then urged supporters to "search for new and different ways to keep making a difference for the people we care about and the causes we cherish."[20]

Defeat didn't change Ann's attitude. She spoke positively about her future during post-election press conferences and cheerfully told listeners that they hadn't seen the last of her. "All the discussions I'm having really have to do with how I might do some things that would

The governor, after admiring a Harley Davidson motorcycle, off-handedly told reporters that she hoped to ride a Harley by the time she reached her sixtieth birthday. The motorcycle company presented an 883 Hugger to the governor during a press conference. She accepted the Harley on behalf of the Department of Public Safety's motorcycle safety unit.

help me make a living," she said at one point. "I'm not going to go away."[21]

She proved this not long afterward by becoming a senior advisor—what some called a "goodwill ambassador"—in the Austin office of a Washington-based law firm. Though she had never been a lawyer, Ann had a lot to offer, based on the experience she had gained from serving in public office.[22]

At a final news conference, Ann said, "I had a fabulous, fabulous four years. I really feel great about those four years." And she added, "Whatever I do, it's going to be wonderful."[23]

All those who have followed Ann through her years in public service can only cheer her on.

Chronology

1933—Dorothy Ann Willis is born in Lakeview, Texas.

1942—With mother, moves to San Diego to join father who was drafted into the Navy.

1945—World War II ends; the Willises return to Texas.

1946—The Willises move to Waco, Texas.

1950—Graduates from Waco High School; enters Baylor University.

1953—Marries David Richards.

1954—Graduates from Baylor University in Waco with major in speech, minor in political science.

1955—Earns teaching certificate from University of Texas at Austin.

1955 —Teaches social studies and history at Fulmore
-1956   Junior High School, Austin, Texas.

1957—Daughter Cecile is born; Ann starts political work.

1959—Son Dan is born.

1962—Son Clark is born; Ann helps found North Dallas Democratic Women and Dallas Committee for Peaceful Integration.

1964—Daughter Ellen is born; Ann continues political work.

1969—The Richardses move to Austin.

1971—Manages Sarah Weddinton's campaign for seat in Texas House of Representatives.

1972—Manages Weddington's House office.
-1974

1974—Helps with Wilhelmina Delco's campaign for state legislature.

1976—Elected Travis County Commissioner.
-1982

1982—Elected Texas State Treasurer.
-1990

1984—Seconds nomination of Walter Mondale for president of the United States; Ann and David are divorced.

1988—Keynote speaker at Democatic National Convention.

1990—Elected governor of Texas.

1992—Was chair of National Democratic Convention in New York City

1994—Runs for reelection; loses race for governor.

Chapter Notes

Preface

1. "Ann Richards," *Current Biography Yearbook*, 1991, (New York: H.W. Wilson Company), p. 470.

2. Ann Richards, "Keynote Address," *Vital Speeches of the Day,* July 1988, Delivered at the National Democratic Convention, Atlanta, Georgia, July 18, 1988, p. 647.

3. Ibid.

4. Fred Astaire and Ginger Rogers were famous film dance partners during the 1930s and 1940s.

Chapter 1

1. Curtis Wilkie, "Read Her Lips," *Boston Globe Magazine*, October 25, 1992, p. 33.

2. Vicki Haddock, "The Wit and Wisdom of Ann Richards," *San Francisco Examiner*, January 27, 1991, p. 3.

3. Al Reinert, "The Titan of Texas," *Vogue*, August 1991, p. 246.

4. Ann Richards with Peter Knobler, *Straight From The Heart—My Life in Politics and Other Places* (New York: Simon and Schuster, 1989), p. 46.

5. Alison Cook, "Lone Star," *New York Times Magazine,* February 7, 1993, p. 27.

6. Reinert, p. 245.

7. Cook, p. 27.

8. Sara Sanborn, "Ann Richards's Success Story," *MS Magazine*, June 1988, p. 88.

9. Reinert, p. 246.

10. Cook, p. 27.

11. Richards/Knobler, p. 47.

Chapter 2

1. Ann Richards with Peter Knobler, *Straight From The Heart—My Life in Politics and Other Places* (New York: Simon and Schuster, 1989), p. 46.

2. "Ann Richards," *Current Biography Yearbook*, 1991 (New York: H.W. Wilson Company), p. 468.

3. Sara Sanborn, "Ann Richards's Success Story," *MS Magazine*, June 1988, p. 88.

4. Mark Donald, "*Cosmo* Talks to Ann Richards, Governor of Texas," *Cosmopolitan*, April 1991, p. 124.

Chapter 3

1. Sara Sanborn, "Ann Richards's Success Story," *MS Magazine*, June 1988, p. 90.

2. Ann Richards with Peter Knobler, *Straight From The Heart—My Life in Politics and Other Places* (New York: Simon and Schuster, 1989), p. 58.

3. Alan Ebert, "Governor Ann Richards: Stay Tuned," *Good Housekeeping*, November 1992, p. 86.

4. Richards/Knobler, p. 60.

5. Ibid.

6. Ann Richards, interview with John Burnett, National Public Radio, "Weekend Edition," May 22, 1993.

7. Richards/Knobler, pp. 62-63.

8. Ebert, p. 87.

9. Sanborn, p. 90.

10. Ebert, p. 86.

11. Al Reinert, "The Titan of Texas," *Vogue*, August 1991, p. 245.

12. Ebert, p. 88.

13. Ibid.

14. Alison Cook, "Lone Star," *New York Times Magazine,* February 7, 1993, p. 29.

Chapter 4

1. Ann Richards with Peter Knobler, *Straight From The Heart—My Life in Politics and Other Places* (New York: Simon and Schuster, 1989), p. 75.

2. Ibid.

3. Mary Conroy, "Ann Richards, Texas Treasurer," *Chicago Tribune,* VI, November 26, 1989, p. 2.

4. Ibid.

5. Sara Sanborn, "Ann Richards's Success Story," *MS Magazine,* June 1988, p. 90.

6. Richards/Knobler, p. 77.

7. Alan Ebert, "Governor Ann Richards: Stay Tuned," *Good Housekeeping,* November 1992, p. 88.

8. Richards/Knobler, p. 81.

9. Sanborn, p. 90.

Chapter 5

1. Carolyn Warner, *The Last Word* (Englewood Cliffs, NJ: Prentice Hall) p. 87.

2. Ann Richards with Peter Knobler, *Straight From The Heart—My Life in Politics and Other Places,* (New York: Simon and Schuster, 1989), p. 83.

3. Celia Morris, *Storming the Statehouse, Running for Governor with Ann Richards and Dianne Feinstein* (New York: Charles Scribner's Sons, 1989) p. 20.

4. Alison Cook, "Lone Star," *New York Times Magazine,* February 7, 1993, p. 39.

5. Morris, p. 21.

6. Curtis Wilkie, "Read Her Lips," *Boston Globe Magazine*, October 25, 1992, p. 38.

Chapter 6

1. Curtis Wilkie, "Read Her Lips," *Boston Globe Magazine*, October 25, 1992, p. 37.

2. Celia Morris, *Storming the Statehouse, Running for Governor with Ann Richards and Dianne Feinstein* (New York: Charles Scribner's Sons, 1989) p. 22.

3. Ann Richards with Peter Knobler, *Straight From The Heart—My Life in Politics and Other Places* (New York: Simon and Schuster, 1989), p. 117.

4. Ibid p. 136.

5. Sara Sanborn, "Ann Richards's Success Story," *MS Magazine*, June 1988, p. 90.

6. Ibid.

7. Al Reinert, "The Titan of Texas," *Vogue*, August 1991, p. 247.

8. Wilkie, p. 42.

9. Reinert, p. 247.

10. Leslie Bennett, "The Many Lives of Ann Richards," *Woman's Day*, October 3, 1989, p. 30.

11. Richards/Knobler, p. 147.

12. Ibid.

13. Morris, p. 300.

14. Sanborn, p. 91.

15. Alan Ebert, "Governor Ann Richards: Stay Tuned," *Good Housekeeping*, November 1992, p. 89.

16. "Ann Richards," *Current Biography Yearbook*, 1991 (New York: H.W. Wilson Company), p. 469.

Chapter 7

1. Al Reinert, "The Titan of Texas," *Vogue*, August 1991, p. 248.

2. Ibid.

3. Sam Attlesey, *Dallas Morning News*, E2, December 5, 1982.

4. Ann Richards with Peter Knobler, *Straight From The Heart—My Life in Politics and Other Places* (New York: Simon and Schuster, 1989), p. 169.

5. "Ann Richards," *Current Biography Yearbook*, 1991 (New York: H.W. Wilson Company), p. 468.

6. Celia Morris, *Storming the Statehouse, Running for Governor with Ann Richards and Dianne Feinstein* (New York: Charles Scribner's Sons, 1989) p. 44.

7. Sara Sanborn, "Ann Richards's Success Story," *MS Magazine*, June 1988, p. 91.

8. Ibid.

9. Richards/Knobler, p. 181.

10. Morris, p. 45.

11. Ibid.

12. Richards/Knobler, p. 202.

13. Ibid.

14. Richards/Knobler, p. 203.

15. Ebert, p. 89.

16. Leslie Bennett, "The Many Lives of Ann Richards," *Woman's Day*, October 3, 1989, p. 34.

17. *Current Biography*, p. 470.

18. Richards/Knobler, p. 205.

19. Ibid.

20. Dave McNeely, "A Lone Star," *D Magazine*, September 1984, p. 50.

21. Ebert, p. 90.

22. Leslie Bennett, "The Many Lives of Ann Richards," *Woman's Day*, October 3, 1989, p. 30.

23. Cook, p. 38.

24. Sanborn, p. 89.

Chapter 8

1. Leslie Bennett, "The Many Lives of Ann Richards," *Woman's Day*, October 3, 1989, p. 32.

2. Sara Sanborn, "Ann Richards's Success Story," *MS Magazine*, June 1988, p. 91.

3. Curtis Wilkie, "Read Her Lips," *Boston Globe Magazine*, October 25, 1992, p. 40.

4. Ann Richards with Peter Knobler, *Straight From The Heart—My Life in Politics and Other Places* (New York: Simon and Schuster, 1989), p. 214.

5. Sanborn, p. 91.

6. Wilkie, p. 39.

7. Alison Cook, "Lone Star," *New York Times Magazine,* February 7, 1993, p. 35.

8. Bennett, p. 32.

9. Celia Morris, *Storming the Statehouse, Running for Governor with Ann Richards and Dianne Feinstein* (New York: Charles Scribner's Sons, 1989) p. 56.

10. Richards/Knobler, p. 217.

11. Richards/Knobler, p. 218.

12. Cook, p. 35.

13. Bennett, p. 33,

14. Cook, p. 41.

15. Kate Northcott, "The Lone Star of Texas," *Ladies Home Journal,* March 1991, p. 64.

16. Ibid.

17. Sanborn, p. 90.

18. Kori Clark, interview with the author, February 3, 1993.

19. Ibid.

20. Ibid.

21. Ibid.

Chapter 9

1. Curtis Wilkie, "Read Her Lips," *Boston Globe Magazine*, October 25, 1992, p. 36.

2. Celia Morris, *Storming the Statehouse, Running for Governor with Ann Richards and Dianne Feinstein*, (New York: Charles Scribner's Sons, 1989) p. 31.

3. Morris, pp. 53-54.

4. Paul Weingarten, "Governor Richards takes Texas by the Horns," *Chicago Tribune*, March 10, 1991, Section 3, p. 5.

5. Marsha Ginsberg, "Richards Goes for Jugular," *San Francisco Examiner*, July 12, 1992, p. A14.

6. Ibid.

7. William Plummer, "After Mud-Slinging Primary, Ann Richards Sets Her Sights On The Lone Star Statehouse," *People Magazine*, April 30, 1990, p. 86.

8. Ginsberg, p. A14.

9. Sam Attlesey, "Richards fights back," *Dallas Morning News*, p. 2.

10. Ginsberg, p. A14.

11. Morris, p. 158-9.

12. Ibid, p. 164.

13. Ibid, p. 161.

14. Wayne Slater and Sam Attlesey, "Richards Takes Texas," *Dallas Morning News*, November 7, 1990, p. 1.

15. Morris, p.1.

16. Al Reinert, "The Titan of Texas," *Vogue*, August 1991, p. 243.

17. Jan Jarbo, "Ann's Plans," *Texas Monthly*, July 1992, p. 124.

18. Morris, p. 4.

19. Ibid.

20. Slater/Attlesey, p. 16.

Chapter 10

1. Kate Northcott, "The Lone Star of Texas," *Ladies Home Journal*, March 1991, p. 64.

2a. John W. Mashek, "Richards Basks in Her Texas Win," *The Boston Globe*, November 8, 1990, p. 33.

2. Mark Donald, "*Cosmo* Talks to Ann Richards, Governor of Texas," *Cosmopolitan*, April 1991, p. 126. 3. Paul Burka, "Ann of a Hundred Days," *Texas Monthly*, March 1991, p. 122.

4. Roberto Suro, "Texas Governor Proves Adept in Her First Year," *New York Times*, January 10, 1992, p. 25.

5. Jarbo, p. 121.

6. Burka, p. 124.

7. Governor's Office Report, 1991-92.

8. Ibid.

9. Suro, p. 25.

10. Kori Clark, interview with the author, March 4, 1993.

11. Ibid.

12. Suro, p. 25.

13. Molly Ivins, "Shrubwacked," (Ivins nicknamed George W. Bush, "Shrub"—from his father), *The Nation*, November 28, 1994, pp. 638-9.

14. "Sonrise," 170 *The Economist*, October 1, 1994.

15. Michael Holmes, "Texas Governor's Race, Nearly Even" (sub-head: Voter Disgust Helps Bush, Hurts Richards), Associated Press, *The Record,* October 6, 1994, p. A38.

16. Ibid.

17. Ken Howard, "Governor's Record One of Quiet Achievements," *Houston Post,* November 9, 1994, p. 15.

18. Sue Anne Pressley, "Texas Ex-governor's Final Garage Sale," *Washington Post,* January 29, 1995, p. A9:1.

19. Ann Richards's post-election thank-you letter to supporters.

20. Ibid.

21. Ken Herman, "Richards Bids Media Farewell," *Houston Post,* December 23, 1994, p. A-1.

22. "Firm Hires Ex-governor," *New York Times,* February 14, 1995.

23. R.G. Ratcliffe, "Richards Sees 'A Wonderful Life' After She Leaves Office," *Houston Chronicle,* November 23, 1994, p. 18A.

Index